Let's Discover The States

Atlantic

DISTRICT OF COLUMBIA • VIRGINIA
WEST VIRGINIA

By
Thomas G. Aylesworth
Virginia L. Aylesworth

CHELSEA HOUSE PUBLISHERS
New York   Philadelphia

Created and produced by Blackbirch Graphics, Inc.

DESIGN: Richard S. Glassman
PROJECT EDITOR: Bruce S. Glassman
ASSOCIATE EDITOR: Robin Langley Sommer

3   5   7   9   8   6   4   2

Printed in the United States

Library of Congress Cataloging-in-Publication Data

Aylesworth, Thomas G.
   The Atlantic.

   (Let's discover the states)
   Includes bibliographies and index.
   Summary: Discusses the geographical, historical, and cultural aspects of Virginia, West Virginia, and Washington D.C.
   1. South Atlantic States—Juvenile literature.   2. Middle Atlantic States—Juvenile literature.   3. Virginia—Juvenile literature.   4. West Virginia—Juvenile literature.   5. Washington (D.C.)—Juvenile literature.   [1. Atlantic States.   2. Virginia.   3. West Virginia.   4. Washington (D.C.)]   I. Aylesworth, Virginia L.   II. Title.   III. Series.

F209.3.A94   1988   975   87-17878
ISBN 1-55546-555-2
   0-7910-0533-X (pbk.)

CONTENTS

WEST VIRGINIA

Lights shining on the gleaming white dome of the
   United States Capitol.
Cherry trees in blossom around the Tidal Basin.
Cobblestone sidewalks along a quiet street in
   Georgetown.
The dignity of Daniel Chester French's monument to
   our best-loved president, the Lincoln Memorial.
Crowds delighted by the antics of the pandas in the
   National Zoo.
A dramatic view of the Mall and the Capitol from the
   Washington Monument.

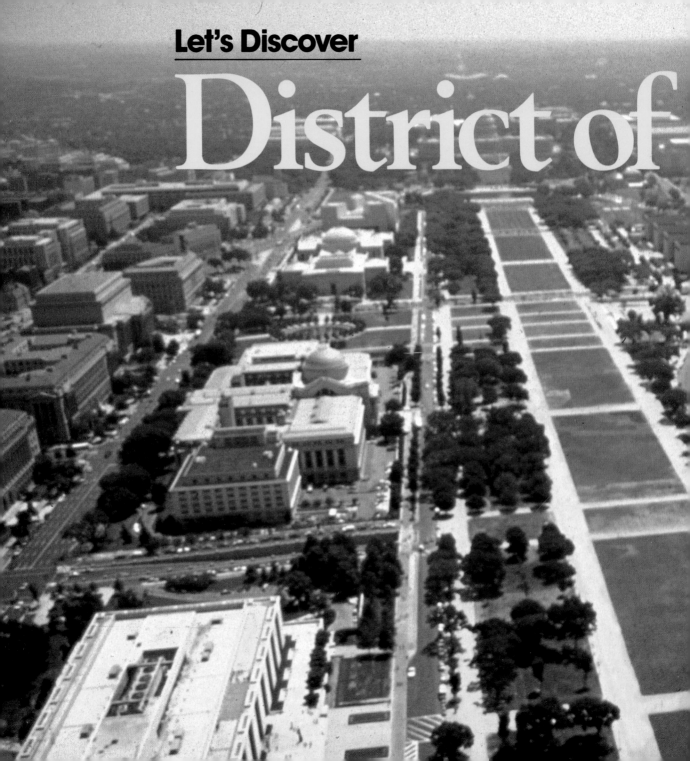

Let's Discover
District of

Columbia

Capital: The city of Washington comprises the District of Columbia,
seat of the federal government of the United States.

THE DISTRICT OF COLUMBIA

At a Glance

Flag

Flower: American Beauty Rose

Major Industries: Government, printing and publishing

Bird: Wood Thrush

Size: 67 square miles

Population: 623,000

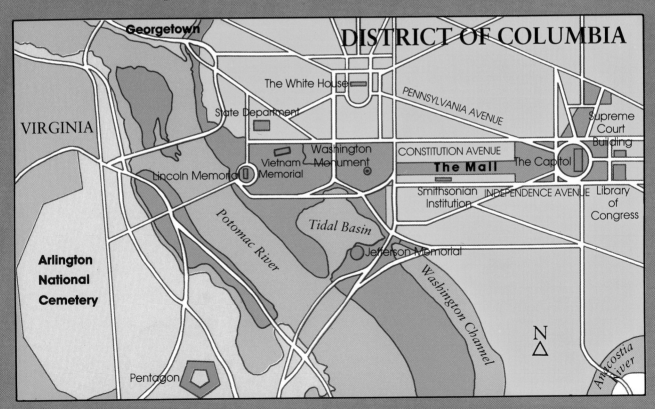

DISTRICT OF COLUMBIA

Georgetown

The White House

State Department

PENNSYLVANIA AVENUE

Supreme Court Building

VIRGINIA

Vietnam Memorial

Washington Monument

Lincoln Memorial

CONSTITUTION AVENUE

The Mall

The Capitol

Smithsonian Institution

INDEPENDENCE AVENUE

Library of Congress

Potomac River

Tidal Basin

Jefferson Memorial

Washington Channel

Arlington National Cemetery

N △

Pentagon

Anacostia River

The city of Washington, D.C. was built along the northeastern shore of the Potomac River, which flows into Chesapeake Bay. The river forms the boundary between the District of Columbia on the east and Virginia on the west.

The Land

The District of Columbia is bordered on the west by Virginia and on the north, east, and south by Maryland. It is within the Atlantic Coastal Plain, which is part of the lowland region that extends north and south along the Atlantic Ocean. This part of the plain is sometimes called the Tidewater, because tidal water flows up its bays, inlets, and rivers.

The District lies along the Potomac River between Maryland and Virginia. Its humid climate results in temperatures between 32 and 50 degrees Fahrenheit in January and 69 to 87 degrees F. in July. Only five to ten inches of snow fall during the winter because of the District's southerly location.

The White House, on Pennsylvania Avenue, is the official residence of the president of the United States. Construction began in 1792. James Hoban designed the building, whose south portico has often been imitated by other architects.

The Supreme Court building is across the street from the Capitol, next to the Library of Congress. As members of the nation's highest court, the nine justices of the Supreme Court are empowered to interpret the Constitution; their rulings have affected the course of American history.

At right:
The Jefferson Memorial, south of the Tidal Basin, was dedicated in 1943, on the 200th anniversary of President Jefferson's birth.

Far right:
Cherry trees in blossom along The Mall with the Washington Monument in the distance.

Below and below right:
The Lincoln Memorial, near the Potomac on the western end of Washington's Mall, houses the famous Daniel Chester French statue of America's best-loved president. The 36 columns comprising the monument's exterior represent the states in the Union at the time of Lincoln's death.

The History

The boundaries of the District of Columbia and the city of Washington are the same. When Europeans arrived in what is now Virginia in the 17th century, the Powhatan Indians were living in some 200 scattered villages in the area. During the early 1700s, some Scottish and Irish trappers and farmers built homes on the east side of the Potomac River in what is now Maryland. Across the river, on the Virginia side, plantations were established, including Mount Vernon, the home of George Washington's family. Washington was largely low-lying swampland at the time.

In 1783 the Continental Congress decided that the new nation needed a federal city to serve as the capital of the United States. But the site of the city was problematic, because of the slavery issue. Slave-holding states in the South did not want the Quaker city of Philadelphia to remain the capital because it was abolitionist. Anti-slavery factions in the North did not want the capital to be in the South, since it might appear that the United States condoned slavery.

Alexander Hamilton and Thomas Jefferson worked out a compromise in 1790 by which Northern representatives agreed to set up a new city on the Potomac River. President Washington seemed the ideal person to select the site, since he had lived in the area for years and was also a former surveyor. Washington persuaded local landowners to sell their holdings on the chosen site to the government for about $66 per acre.

The original plans called for a capital exactly 10 miles square on land taken from the states of Maryland and Virginia. In 1791 the purchase of the land from private owners was completed. Washington and an ingenious young French engineer, Major Pierre Charles L'Enfant, set up planning headquarters in a small stone cottage in Georgetown. The city of Washington, named for the president, would be the first planned for a specific purpose.

L'Enfant chose a flat-topped hill, now known as Capitol Hill, as the site of the United States Capitol. L'Enfant's vision was impressive: it called for great avenues, expansive parks, and at least one boulevard a full 400 feet wide. Plans were progressing well, and buildings were on their way up—Washington himself would lay the Capitol cornerstone in 1793. But L'Enfant's enthusiasm for spaciousness ran away with him. He demanded that a wealthy and influential District citizen move out of the path of a planned boulevard—then demolished his new manor house when he refused to comply. Washington was forced to dismiss the young Frenchman, who was replaced by Benjamin Banneker, a distinguished black architect and astronomer, and Andrew Ellicott.

Two years into the War of 1812, British forces invaded Washington and burned every public building except the post office. Plans to protect the capital had proved inadequate, and the city was in ruins until peace came in 1815.

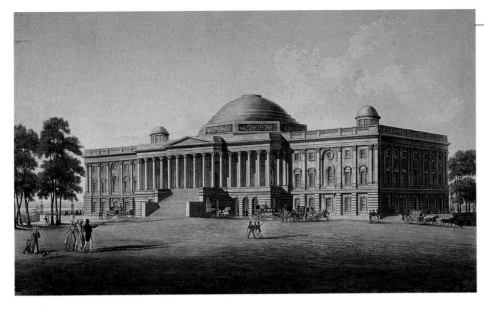

The U.S. Capitol in 1824. Its construction was interrupted repeatedly between 1793, when President George Washington laid the cornerstone, and 1850, when the building was completed.

The basic concept was L'Enfant's, but preserving it has not been easy. For one thing, not all heads of government have shared his reverence for clear-spaced grandeur. Andrew Jackson, for example, is rumored to have planted the great gray Treasury Building directly in the way of a planned White House-Capitol vista with an arbitrary wave of his cane. Another problem was construction stoppages due to chronic lack of funds. Although work on the Capitol began in 1793, the permanent 4,500-ton cast-iron dome was not in place for Lincoln's 1861 inaugural; work on the Washington Monument stood still for 20 years—a fact permanently reflected in its two-toned marble facing.

In the beginning, Congress planned to build the rest of the government buildings on the high plateau east of the Capitol. But when they tried to buy the land, it had been purchased by speculators who were going to charge too much money. So Congress changed its plans and bought the marshy ground west of the Capitol. The north section of the Capitol was completed in 1800, and Congress held its first session in the building in November of that year. President John Adams had moved to Washington from Philadelphia five months earlier.

The City of Washington was incorporated in 1802. (The District of Columbia was created as a municipal corporation in 1871, comprising Washington, Georgetown, and Washington County.) In 1814, during the War of 1812, British forces captured Washington and burned the Capitol, the White House, and other government buildings, but their reconstruction was complete by 1819. Washington's economy and population began growing rapidly, as the demands of government increased. But for many years, District development remained well within its original geographical boundaries. In fact, 50 years after its original purchase, Virginia's land was returned, unused, to its original owners.

The first great expansion of Washington occurred during the Civil War. Confederate forces tried to capture the capital repeatedly, and large Union armies had to be quartered in unsightly temporary buildings. In 1871 Congress approved funds to replace these buildings and to improve the appearance of the city.

William Henry Harrison, the ninth president of the United States, was inaugurated on the steps of the Capitol in 1841. As the city of Washington grew larger and more sophisticated during the 1800s, it assumed its rightful place as a focal point of the nation's intellectual, social, and cultural life.

The capital's second major expansion came during World War I, when carpenters put up what were intended to be temporary buildings along Constitution Avenue to provide office space for additional wokers. Some of these buildings still stand. Washington increased in both size and importance again during the Great Depression of the 1930s, when the federal government became the primary agent of relief and recovery. Many new office buildings were constructed for increasing activities, but even these could not hold all the workers who arrived in Washington during World War II. Government had become big business, and Washington's population spilled over into Maryland and Virginia. This expansion continues today.

Pennsylvania Avenue, which connects the White House to the Capitol, was designed as the city's major thoroughfare. In 1865 some 30,000 people thronged the avenue for the funeral procession of Abraham Lincoln.

17

In 1804 Congress passed a law establishing Washington's first public elementary school. Georgetown University, founded in 1789, was already in operation. By the turn of the 20th century, there were eight other institutions of higher education in the District of Columbia: George Washington University (1821), Gallaudet College for the deaf (1864), Howard University (1867), Catholic University of America (1887), St. Joseph's Seminary of Washington, D.C. (1888), St. Paul's College (1889), American University (1893), and Trinity College (1897). Washington's Library of Congress is the largest library in the United States, with a collection of more than 35 million items.

In 1963 thousands of Americans took part in the Freedom March on Washington, led by Martin Luther King, Jr. Demonstrators converged on the capital to show their support for racial equality and full civil rights for all Americans.

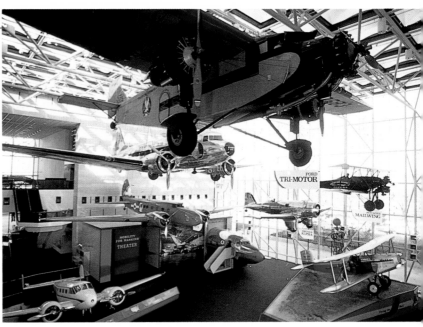

The People

More than 93 percent of Washington's citizens were born in the United States, but Washington is truly a cosmopolitan city, with residents representing almost every nation and all 50 states of the Union.

Statesmen, military leaders, and government officials too numerous to mention have made their homes in Washington, D.C., although most of them came from other parts of the country. Such writers as Walt Whitman, the author of *Leaves of Grass* and other outstanding books of poetry, have also lived in the nation's capital. Julia Ward Howe composed the "Battle Hymn of the Republic" in Washington, and John Philip Sousa led the U.S. Marine Band in the late 1800s and composed "The Stars and Stripes Forever." Portraits by Charles Wilson Peale, Gilbert Stuart, and Thomas Sully adorn the Capitol. Jazz composer, conductor, and pianist Duke Ellington was born in the District of Columbia, and actresses Helen Hayes, Chita Rivera, and Goldie Hawn also came from Washington.

Above left:
In 1846 James Smithson, an Englishman, left his entire fortune to the United States for the establishment of the Smithsonian Institution in Washington. This bequest, "for the increase and diffusion of knowledge among men," helped make the nation's capital a center for learning and scientific research.

Above:
The National Air and Space Museum of the Smithsonian exhibits antique aircraft and scale models of rockets and space vehicles.

The Vietnam Veterans Memorial.

OF SPECIAL INTEREST

ON CAPITOL HILL: *The United States Capitol*
The stately five-story meeting place of Congress, crowned by a 259-foot-high dome, extends over some 3½ acres.

ON THE MALL: *The Smithsonian Institution*
The Smithsonian's complex of buildings houses fascinating exhibits on natural and American history, space, art, and much more. Its collection is so extensive that it is called "the nation's attic."

ON THE MALL: *The Lincoln Memorial*
The majestic Lincoln Memorial is dominated by Daniel Chester French's imposing white Georgian marble statue of President Lincoln.

DOWNTOWN: *Ford's Theatre*
This restored theater was the scene of Abraham Lincoln's assassination. It now houses a museum of more than 3,000 Lincoln items.

IN THE NORTHWEST: *Embassy Section*
Surrounding and north of Sheridan Circle N.W. and the intersection of Massachusetts Avenue and 23rd Street N.W. are dozens of foreign legations, many with striking architecture.

For more information write:
WASHINGTON CONVENTION AND VISITORS ASSOCIATION
1575 EYE STREET N.W., SUITE 250
WASHINGTON, D.C. 20005

FURTHER READING

Aylesworth, Thomas G. and Virginia L. *Washington: The Nation's Capital.* Gallery Books, 1986.

Duffield, Judy, and others. *Washington, D.C.: The Complete Guide*, Random House, 1982.

Froncek, Thomas, ed. *The City of Washington: An Illustrated History.* Alfred A. Knopf, 1977.

Gutheim, Fredrick A. *The Federal City: Plans and Realities.* Smithsonian Institution, 1976.

Lewis, David L. *District of Columbia: A Bicentennial History.* W.W. Norton, 1976.

The sweeping lawns and imposing mansion at Mount
 Vernon—the home of George Washington.
An early morning mist in the Blue Ridge Mountains.
Stately Monticello, designed by Thomas Jefferson as
 his home.
A fife-and-drum parade at Williamsburg.
The serenity of wooded Natural Bridge near
 Lexington.
Cool sea breezes blowing in from the Atlantic.

Let's Discover
Virginia

VIRGINIA

At a Glance

State Bird: Cardinal

Capital: Richmond

State Flag

Major Industries: Textiles, transportation equipment, chemicals, government

Major Crops: Tobacco, soybeans, peanuts, corn

State Flower: Flowering Dogwood

KENTUCKY

JEFFERSON NATIONAL FOREST

TENNESSEE

Size: 40,817 square miles (36th largest)

Population: 5,636,000 (13th largest)

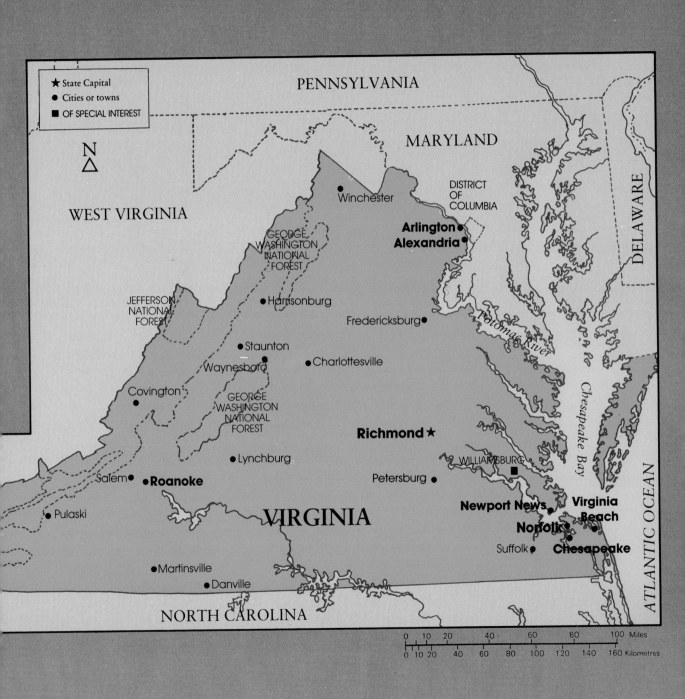

PENNSYLVANIA

MARYLAND

WEST VIRGINIA

DISTRICT
OF
COLUMBIA

★ State Capital
● Cities or towns
■ OF SPECIAL INTEREST

N
△

DELAWARE

Winchester

Arlington ●
Alexandria ●

GEORGE
WASHINGTON
NATIONAL
FOREST

JEFFERSON
NATIONAL
FOREST

● Harrisonburg

Fredericksburg ●

Potomac River

● Staunton

Waynesboro

● Charlottesville

Covington ●

GEORGE
WASHINGTON
NATIONAL
FOREST

Chesapeake Bay

Richmond ★

WILLIAMSBURG ■

● Lynchburg

Petersburg ●

Salem ● **Roanoke**

Newport News ●

**Virginia
Beach**

VIRGINIA

Norfolk ●

● Pulaski

Suffolk ●

Chesapeake

ATLANTIC OCEAN

● Martinsville

● Danville

NORTH CAROLINA

0 10 20   40   60   80   100 Miles
0 10 20   40   60   80   100   120   140 160 Kilometres

The Land

Virginia is bordered on the west by Kentucky and West Virginia; on the north by West Virginia, the District of Columbia, and Maryland; on the east by Maryland and the Atlantic Ocean; and on the south by North Carolina. The state has five main land regions: the Appalachian Plateau, the Appalachian Ridge and Valley Region, the Blue Ridge, the Piedmont, and the Atlantic Coastal Plain.

The Appalachian Plateau consists of a rugged strip in southwestern Virginia with an average elevation of some 2,000 feet above sea level. The area has many streams, some of which have cut deep gorges, and large stands of timber. Coal is mined here.

The Appalachian Ridge and Valley Region extends along most of Virginia's western border. It is a series of parallel mountain ridges with broad valleys between them. The region contains many caves and unusual rock formations that were created by the action of water on limestone. Beef and dairy cattle, sheep, poultry, and fruit are raised here, and gypsum, stone, and clay are quarried.

The Blue Ridge borders the Appalachian Ridge on the east and is part of the larger Appalachian Mountain system. The state's highest point, Mount Rogers, 5,729 feet high, is located here. Tobacco, corn, and fruit are among the region's crops.

Above right:
The Shenandoah River Valley is the largest single valley in Virginia. Its fertile soil and temperate climate are well suited to many types of farming.

Above:
Part of southwestern Virginia lies within the Appalachian Plateau. Rugged terrain, rocky ridges, and narrow gorges form the landscape of this region.

26

The Piedmont is in central Virgina. This is the largest land region in the state, consisting of an elevated plain with low hills. Hay, vegetables, fruit, and corn are grown in the region.

The Atlantic Coastal Plain, about 100 miles wide in Virginia, is adjacent to the Atlantic Ocean on the east. It is part of a larger coastal formation along the eastern United States and is sometimes called the Tidewater because of its many inlets, salt marshes, and swamps. Soybeans, berries, and vegetables grow in this region, and fish, crabs, and oysters come from the coastal waters.

The coastline of Virginia is 112 miles long, but if the small bays and inlets are included, it measures 3,315 miles. The state's major waterways are the Rappahannock, James, York, Potomac, Shenandoah, Roanoke, and New Rivers. The largest lake in the state is Lake Drummond, in the Dismal Swamp.

There are few extremes of temperature in Virginia, with averages running from 32 to 50 degrees Fahrenheit in January and from 69 to 87 degrees F. in July, depending upon proximity to the ocean. Snowfall ranges between 25 and 30 inches in the western mountains, with as little as 5 to 10 inches in the Tidewater area.

Tobacco is Virginia's most valuable crop. The state ranks fourth in the nation in tobacco production.

Virginia Beach, on the state's southeastern coast, is one of the East's most popular summer resorts.

The History

When European explorers first came to the Virginia territory, Indian tribes living there spoke three different languages. The Powhatan, members of the Algonquian language group, lived along the coast. In the Piedmont region were the Monacan and the Manahoac, who spoke the Siouan language. Other Siouan-speaking tribes lived along the James and Roanoke Rivers. The Iroquoian language family was represented by the Susquehanna, near the upper Chesapeake Bay, and some smaller tribes.

The first European explorers to arrive in what would become Virginia were probably Spanish Jesuit priests who established a short-lived mission on the York River in 1570. Fourteen years later, Sir Walter Raleigh was given a charter by Queen Elizabeth I of England to establish colonies in North America. Raleigh sent some settlers to the New World, but the expeditions failed because of lack of supplies. It was Raleigh who named the area Virginia, for Elizabeth, who was called the Virgin Queen.

On May 14, 1607, settlers from the Virginia Company of London established the first permanent English colony in America on a peninsula along the James River. Members of the settlement, called Jamestown, hoped to reap profits from trade with the Indians. But harsh winter weather, disease, hunger, and Indian attacks almost discouraged the first colonists from staying in Virginia.

Pocahontas, the daughter of Chief Powhatan, was a child of 10 or 12 when the English settled at Jamestown. Allegedly, she saved the life of colonial leader Captain John Smith when he was captured by the confederation headed by her father. Later, Pocahontas was taken hostage by a band of Englishmen who wanted to exchange her for English prisoners. While she was being detained in Jamestown, colonist John Rolfe fell in love with her and obtained permission from the governor for their marriage, which took place in 1614.

King James I of England set up the Virginia Company of London (sometimes called the London Company) in 1606 to organize the colonization of Virginia. The company sent settlers who established the first permanent English settlement in America at Jamestown in 1607, under the leadership of Captain John Smith. The colonists had a hard life, but managed to survive.

Smith was injured in 1609 and had to return to England. The following winter, lack of food began to take its toll, and many settlers died. But in the spring, English ships arrived with fresh supplies and new colonists.

In 1612 John Rolfe, one of the colonists, began to raise tobacco, which may have saved the colony. Exporting cured tobacco gave the people a new way of supporting themselves. Rolfe married Pocahontas, the daughter of the Indian chief Powhatan, in 1614, and the marriage brought peace between the Indians and the colonists for a time.

By 1619 each settler had land of his own, and the Virginia Company decided to send boatloads of young women as wives for the settlers. That year the House of Burgesses, the first representative legislature in America, was formed in Virginia. Dutch traders brought the first slaves to Jamestown, and Virginians built a plantation economy on slave labor. A landed aristocracy emerged.

Farmers had begun to settle as far west as the edge of the Piedmont by 1650. They resented the fact that the territory was being run by the aristocrats of the Tidewater area. They also resented British laws that limited colonial trade. In 1676 a group of dissenters commanded by the young planter Nathaniel Bacon carried out an armed rebellion. Bacon's Rebellion was the first uprising of its kind in the British colonies. After a series of victories over the repressive governor Sir William Berkeley, and a few minor legislative advances, Bacon suddenly died of malaria. Without its leader, the rebellion collapsed and brought no essential political change to the colony.

In 1699 the capital of Virginia was moved from Jamestown to Williamsburg, and by 1700, English settlers had penetrated west to the mountains. The French, who had claimed the western part of the territory, resented this, and the fourth French and Indian War broke out in 1754. The British defeated the French and their Indian allies, and England controlled the region after 1763.

In the early 1770s, the Indians were attacking settlers who moved into their lands along Virginia's western frontier, which led to Lord Dunmore's War. The conflict was named for the governor of Virginia, John Murray, Earl of Dunmore. Virginia soldiers commanded by Andrew Lewis defeated the Shawnee Indians at Point Pleasant (which is now in West Virginia) in 1774, and the threat of Indian raids decreased.

Virginia's upper class had time for scholarship, for the development and debate of ideas, and for independent thinking. A remarkable group of leaders emerged: the eloquent Patrick Henry, George Washington, the versatile Thomas Jefferson, James Madison, and James Monroe, whose impression on our political philosophy is

George Washington was born in Westmoreland County, in 1732. From this small house on the Potomac, one of America's greatest leaders would emerge.

George Washington distinguished himself early in life as a member of Virginia society. The son of a wealthy planter, young Washington was 16 when he began his career as a land surveyor in the Shenandoah Valley. After gaining a knowledge of the wilderness and experience with the Indians, Washington joined his state's militia. His leadership abilities resulted in a remarkable rise to command during the colonial wars and the American Revolution.

indelible. Virginia would furnish the new United States with four of its first five presidents.

Strong leadership resulted in independent action. In 1774 the British Parliament ordered the port of Boston closed as punishment for the Boston Tea Party. The Virginia House of Burgesses made the day of closing a day of fasting and prayer in support of the Massachusetts colonists. As a result, Governor Dunmore dissolved the House of Burgesses. The members then met without permission

in Williamsburg, calling themselves the First Virginia Convention. They elected delegates to the First Continental Congress.

The Second Virginia Convention was held in March 1775 in Richmond, where Patrick Henry made the famous speech in which he said, "Give me liberty or give me death!" The Second Continental

Virginia-born Patrick Henry was one of the most influential orators and statesmen of the American Revolution. His speeches aroused strong public support for action against the British.

Thomas Jefferson was one of Virginia's exceptionally talented native sons. In addition to writing the Declaration of Independence and serving as the third president of the United States, Jefferson was a respected diplomat, educator, architect, inventor, and gourmet.

On October 19, 1781, after fighting his way onto the peninsula between the York and James Rivers, British lieutenant general Charles Cornwallis was forced to surrender to George Washington at Yorktown. The British force had been cut off by a French fleet, and its defeat effectively ended the Revolutionary War, although the British government did not recognize the new republic until the Treaty of Paris was signed in September 1783.

Congress met later that year and elected George Washington commander in chief of the Continental Army. In 1776 Virginia adopted its first constitution and became an independent commonwealth. Patrick Henry was named governor, and Lord Dunmore was expelled from the colony. The capital was moved from Williamsburg to Richmond in 1780.

During the Revolutionary War, there was a higher percentage of revolutionaries in Virginia than in any other southern colony. Thomas Jefferson wrote the Declaration of Independence in 1776. Virginia contributed the cavalry leader "Light-Horse Harry" Lee and Daniel Morgan, the hero of the battles of Saratoga and Cowpens. Another prominent Virginian, George Rogers Clark, won Revolutionary War victories in the Northwest Territory (roughly the present-day Midwest). In 1781 the final victory of the Revolution was achieved at Yorktown, when Lord Cornwallis surrendered to George Washington.

Virginia ratified the new Constitution of the United States in 1788 and became the tenth state of the Union. In 1792 the westernmost counties of Virginia became the state of Kentucky.

Thomas "Stonewall" Jackson was one of the Confederacy's ablest and most respected military leaders. He won his nickname when his brigade held firmly against the great Union assault at the First Battle of Bull Run, where a fellow officer inspired his men to rally by shouting "There is Jackson standing like a stone wall!"

Robert E. Lee, born in Stratford in 1807, was the South's greatest Civil War general. He commanded Confederate forces from May 1862 until the war ended in 1865. A brilliant strategist, Lee fought in most of the war's major battles, including Fredericksburg, Chancellorsville, Gettysburg, and Appomattox Court House, the scene of his surrender to Union general Ulysses S. Grant.

During the Mexican War of 1846 to 1848, Virginia military leaders including Thomas J. Jackson, Joseph E. Johnston, Robert E. Lee, and Winfield Scott distinguished themselves and gained experience that would soon be needed in the Civil War. The paradox of Virginia's history—one of fighters for freedom whose economy depended on slavery—became apparent in 1861. Virginia was not in favor of leaving the Union before the Civil War, but when President Lincoln called for volunteers to stop the secession movement, Virginia formed her own volunteer army, led by Robert E. Lee, and seceded from the Union. Many western counties opposed this decision and maintained a government loyal to the Union. In 1863 48 of these counties formed the state of West Virginia.

The majority of Civil War battles were fought on Virginia soil. Southern victories were achieved at the first and second battles of Bull Run (Manassas), during "Stonewall" Jackson's Valley Campaign, and at Fredericksburg and Chancellorsville. Richmond, the Confederate capital, was assaulted repeatedly by Union troops,

Yorktown was the site of a bloody Civil War battle in 1862. This print depicts the bombardment of Confederate troops by Union forces. The siege forced the Southern army to retreat and withdraw to Richmond.

The end of the Civil War: General Robert E. Lee surrenders to Ulysses S. Grant at Appomattox Court House, Virginia, on April 9, 1865.

and the Shenandoah Valley was hotly contested because it supplied food for Confederate armies. Ironclad warships fought for the first time at Hampton Roads, where the Union's *Monitor* and the *Merrimack* (renamed *Virginia* by the Confederate Navy) clashed in 1862. Like the Revolutionary War, the Civil War ended in Virginia, with Lee's surrender to General Ulysses S. Grant at Appomattox on April 9, 1865.

After the war, the ravaged state of Virginia began again, with nothing on which to rebuild her fortunes. Virginia was not readmitted to the Union until 1870, after five years of military occupation by federal forces and political domination by the Radical Republicans of the Reconstruction era. During the 1880s, the state began to develop some industrial and agricultural diversity with the establishment of cigarette factories, textile plants, and shipyards. But opportunities were few, and thousands of people left the state—a pattern that continued into the early 1900s.

Unlike most states, Virginia benefited from the Great Depression of the 1930s in the form of federal programs that created new jobs and helped stem the outgoing flow of population. Then World War II, which the United States entered in 1941, brought thousands of servicemen, shipbuilders, and government officials, especially into the area around Washington, D.C., and Norfolk. Many of these people settled in Virginia after the war ended in 1945.

Postwar improvements in Virginia included extensive highway construction and completion of the Chesapeake Bay Bridge–Tunnel linking the Norfolk area with the Eastern Shore. Industrial growth in the clothing, metals, and machinery fields strengthened Virginia's economy, and tourism became a $4 billion business. Virginia's scenic Skyline Drive, seashore resorts, historic sites, and other attractions draw visitors from all over the country.

Virginia had the first free schools in what is now the United States: the Syms Free School, founded at Hampton in 1634, and the Easton Free School in the same community, founded in 1640. Virginia's state-wide public school system began in 1870. The first institution of higher education in Virginia was the College of William and Mary. It was founded in 1693, and is the second oldest university in the United States. By the time Virginia entered the Union in 1788, two other colleges and universities had been established: what is now Washington and Lee University (1749) and Hampden-Sydney College (1776).

At right:
Cyrus McCormick, born near Lexington, Virginia, invented the first successful mechanical reaper in 1831 and revolutionized the agricultural industry.

Far right:
Confederate cavalry leader J. E. B. (Jeb) Stuart was born in Patrick County. After distinguishing himself in daring cavalry raids against Union forces, Stuart briefly took command of Stonewall Jackson's corps at Chancellorsville in 1863.

The People

Some 66 percent of the people in Virginia live in towns and cities such as Richmond, Lynchburg, Norfolk, and Arlington. Most of them were born in the United States. The largest religious groups in the state are the Southern Baptists and the Methodists. Other sizable denominations are the National Baptists, Roman Catholics, Presbyterians, and Episcopalians.

Virginia is often called "the Land of Presidents," because no fewer than eight of our chief executives were born there. In order of their terms of office, they were George Washington (the first president), born in Westmoreland County; Thomas Jefferson (third), born in Shadwell; James Madison (fourth), born in King George County; James Monroe (fifth), born in Westmoreland County; William Henry Harrison (ninth) and John Tyler (tenth), born in Charles City County; Zachary Taylor (twelfth), born in Orange County; and Woodrow Wilson (twenty-eighth), born in Staunton.

Other prominent patriots and military leaders from the Old Dominion include the orator Patrick Henry (Studley); one of the great chief justices of the United States, John Marshall (Germantown); and Generals Robert E. Lee (Stratford), Henry "Light-Horse Harry" Lee (Prince William County), and James E. B. "Jeb" Stuart (Patrick County).

The first man to fly over both the North and South Poles was a Virginian—explorer Richard E. Byrd, a native of Winchester. The army doctor who conquered yellow fever, Walter Reed, was born in Belroi. The distinguished black educator Booker T. Washington came from Franklin County. Celebrated novelist Willa Cather, author of the Pulitzer Prize-winning *One of Ours, O Pioneers, My Antonia,* and other works, was born in Winchester.

In the field of popular music, Virginia has contributed singers Ella Fitzgerald (Newport News) and Wayne Newton (Norfolk). Actors and actresses from Virginia include Warren Beatty and his sister, Shirley MacLaine (Richmond), and George C. Scott (Wise). The great professional football quarterback Fran Tarkenton was born in Richmond.

Far left:
Booker T. Washington, founder of Tuskegee Institute, a black college in Alabama, was born near Hale's Ford in 1856.

At left:
Rear Admiral Richard E. Byrd, born in Winchester, pioneered the aerial exploration of both the North and South Poles and opened the frozen continent of Antarctica to further exploration.

Virginia: Land of Presidents

George Washington, 1st president of the United States, known as "father of Our Country," was born in Wakefield.

The 3rd president of the United States, Thomas Jefferson, was born in Albermarle County.

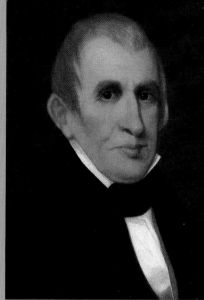

James Madison, a native of Port Conway, was America's 4th president.

James Monroe, the 5th president, was born in Westmoreland County.

The nation's 9th president, William Henry Harrison, came from Berkeley.

John Tyler, a native of Greenway, was the 10th president.

America's 12th president, Zachary Taylor, was born in Orange County.

Woodrow Wilson, our nation's 28th president, was born in Staunton.

41

Mount Vernon.

Monticello.

Arlington National Cemetery.

OF SPECIAL INTEREST

IN WILLIAMSBURG: *Colonial Williamsburg*
The second colonial capital of Virginia has been restored to look as it did in the 1700s, with antique furnishings, horse-drawn carriages, and guides in period costume.

NEAR WASHINGTON, D.C.: *Mount Vernon*
George Washington's gracious Virginia home was built by his father about 1735.

IN RICHMOND: *St. John's Episcopal Church*
It was in this church that Patrick Henry made his impassioned plea for "liberty or death" on the eve of the Revolutionary War.

NEAR CHARLOTTESVILLE: *Monticello*
Thomas Jefferson's estate, which he designed himself, is one of Virginia's landmarks.

IN ARLINGTON: *Arlington National Cemetery*
The most famous of our national cemeteries, Arlington contains the Tomb of the Unknown Soldier, the grave of President John F. Kennedy, and Arlington House, where Robert E. Lee lived.

For more information write:
VIRGINIA STATE TRAVEL SERVICE
202 NORTH 9TH STREET, SUITE 500
RICHMOND, VIRGINIA 23219

FURTHER READING

Carpenter, Allan. *Virginia*, rev. ed. Childrens Press, 1978.
Dabney, Virginius. *Virginia: The New Dominion*. Doubleday, 1971.
Fradin, Dennis B. *Virginia in Words and Pictures*. Childrens Press, 1976.
Friddell, Guy. *We Began at Jamestown*. Dietz Press, 1968.
Rouse, Parke, *Virginia: A Pictorial History*. Scribners, 1975.
Rubin, Louis D., Jr. *Virginia: A Bicentennial History*. W.W. Norton, 1977.

Roaring water cascading over Blackwater Falls.
Autumn foliage on the hills of the Appalachian Plateau.
A sternwheel towboat pushing a barge along the
    Kanawha River.
The artistry of craftsmen etching beautiful designs into
    blown glass.
Echoes from the past in Harpers Ferry National
    Historical Park.

Let's Discover

West

Virginia

WEST VIRGINIA
At a Glance

Capital: Charleston

State Flower: Rhododendron

Major Industries: Machinery, paper and wood products

Major Crops: Corn, beans, beets, hay, oats, cabbage

Size: 24,181 square miles (41st largest)

Population: 1,952,000 (34th largest)

State Bird: Cardinal

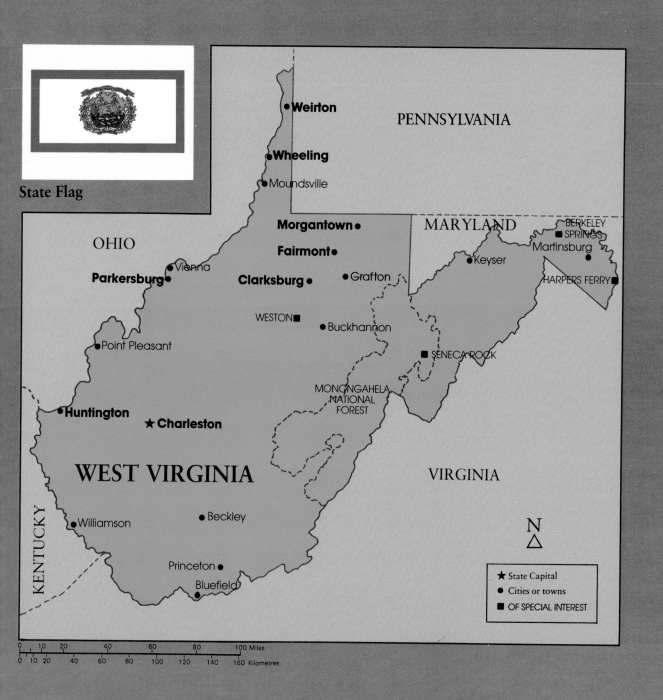

State Flag

PENNSYLVANIA

● **Weirton**

● **Wheeling**

● Moundsville

OHIO

● **Morgantown**

MARYLAND

BERKELEY
■ SPRINGS

Martinsburg ●

● **Fairmont**

● Vienna

Parkersburg ●

● Keyser

Clarksburg ●

● Grafton

HARPERS FERRY ■

WESTON ■

● Buckhannon

● Point Pleasant

■ SENECA ROCK

MONONGAHELA
NATIONAL
FOREST

● **Huntington**

★ **Charleston**

WEST VIRGINIA

VIRGINIA

KENTUCKY

● Williamson

● Beckley

N
△

Princeton ●

★ State Capital

Bluefield ●

● Cities or towns

■ OF SPECIAL INTEREST

0	10	20		40		60		80		100 Miles
0	10	20	40	60	80	100	120	140		160 Kilometres

The Land

West Virginia is bordered on the west by Kentucky and Ohio; on the north by Ohio, Pennyslvania, and Maryland; on the east by Maryland and Virginia; and on the south by Virginia. The state has three main land regions: the Appalachian Ridge and Valley Region, the Appalachian Plateau, and the Blue Ridge.

The Appalachian Ridge and Valley Region covers a wide strip along the eastern border of West Virginia. The Allegheny Mountains, part of the Appalachian system, are located here. Their peaks alternate with valleys where swift streams make their way through the sedimentary rock that underlies the region. Caves are common, and the moutainsides are forested. Hogs, poultry, sheep, and dairy and beef cattle are raised in the area, which also has coal mines and sand and gravel quarries.

The Allegheny Highlands, in eastern West Virginia, have thick forests, beautiful peaks, and fertile valleys.

The Cumberland Mountain region lies west of the Allegheny Highlands. This scenic area includes forested hills, tablelands, and streams.

The Appalachian Plateau covers most of the state west of the Appalachian Ridge and Valley Region. This is rugged country with narrow valleys, flat-topped uplands, and rounded hills. Many mountains in the northwestern section are more than 4,000 feet above sea level. Most of the state's coal, salt, oil, and natural gas deposits are located here. It is also a region of dairy and beef-cattle farms, fruit and vergetable crops, and vineyards.

Much of West Virginia is mountainous, and its rugged hills contain many mineral resources.

The Blue Ridge Mountains touch West Virginia at the tip of the Eastern Panhandle. Their slopes and valleys support apple and peach orchards on fertile soil overlying the igneous (fire-formed) rock that occurs in this part of the Appalachian system.

Summer temperatures in West Virginia average 74 degrees Fahrenheit in the valley regions; 68 degrees F. is the norm for the mountains. In January, temperatures rarely fall below 29 degrees F. in the mountains and are slightly higher in the valleys. Rainfall averages 44 inches yearly, with snowfall varying from 20 to 35 inches throughout the state.

The History

The first residents of what would become West Virginia were the ancient mound builders—the Adena people of 2,000 to 3,000 years ago and their successors, the Hopewell, of 1,500 to 2,000 years ago. They constructed great mounds of earth that were ceremonial sites and smaller mounds in which they buried their dead. They practiced agriculture, knew how to make pottery, and carved useful and ritual objects from soft stone. Many of their earthworks can still be seen at Moundsville, in the Northern Panhandle, and in the Great Kanawha Valley. Excavations have uncovered elaborately adorned human skeletons and artifacts of great beauty.

When European explorers arrived in the 1670s, the mound builders had long since vanished, and the area was a hunting ground for several Indian tribes from the north and east. The Cherokee, Conoy, Delaware, Shawnee, and Susquehanna came into the mountainous region to hunt during the summer and gathered salt from pools of brine.

Present-day West Virginia was part of the territory granted to the London Company by King James I of England for the Virginia colony in 1606. Its remoteness discouraged settlement, and the first non-Indian to visit the region was probably the German explorer John Lederer and his companions, who reached the Blue Ridge in 1669. Two years later, Thomas Batts and Robert Fallam came into the region in search of furs and transportation routes.

Morgan ap Morgan of Delaware, who moved into the Bunker Hill section of the Eastern Panhandle in 1726, is credited with being the first permanent colonial settler. Others soon followed, many of them Germans from Pennsylvania, who established a settlement called New Mecklenburg (now Shepherdstown) in 1727. Other newcomers were Welsh and Scots-Irish farmers who settled in the Eastern Panhandle, the Ohio Valley, and along the Greenbrier and New Rivers.

The Indians resisted these encroachments into their territory by raiding settlements. To defend themselves, the pioneers built forts and blockhouses, some of which grew into towns and cities. Among them were Forts Henry (now Wheeling), Lee (now Charleston), and Randolph (now Point Pleasant). During the French and Indian Wars, the British fought the French and their Indian allies for control of the region. In 1754 George Washington led an unsuccessful raid against the French in what is now West Virginia, and the following year the French and Indians defeated British general Edward Braddock in a number of battles.

Coal was discovered in 1742 and would eventually become a major source of revenue for the state, but only after railroads began expanding in the mid-1800s. Lumber became important after 1755, with the advent of water-powered sawmills.

King George III refused, in 1763, to let the colonists settle on land west of the Alleghenies until treaties could be made with the Indians, but many Virginia pioneers ignored these orders and moved west. In 1768 treaties were signed with the Cherokee and the Iroquoian-speaking Mingo, and by 1775, some 30,000 settlers were living between the Allegheny Mountains and the Ohio River. These people were far from the seat of Virginia government at Williamsburg, and they began to demand their own government as early as 1776. Meanwhile, George Washington's brother, Charles, had laid out the city of Charles Town, which was named for him, in 1768. The town of Bath, a health resort at Berkeley Springs, had been established two years earlier.

The western settlers sent many men to fight in the Revolutionary War. Indian armies led by British officers invaded the area three times between 1777 and 1782, but they were repulsed. Industry began to develop even during the Revolution, and after the war ended in 1783, the first iron furnace west of the Alleghenies was built in the Northern Panhandle. In 1808 the Kanawha Valley began producing large quantities of salt, and the nation's first natural gas well was discovered at Charleston in 1815.

James Wilson accidently discovered the nation's first natural gas well at Charleston in 1815. The discovery offered a major opportunity for West Virginia's economy to expand and prosper.

Harper's Ferry (then in Virginia) was the site of John Brown's unsuccessful 1859 raid on the federal arsenal there.

During the early 1800s, western settlers felt increasingly estranged from eastern Virginians. The easterners owned large plantations and used the Atlantic Ocean for commerce. The westerners were primarily small farmers who carried out trade on the waterways flowing toward the Mississippi River. They felt that their interests were ignored by the state government, and bitter disputes broke out over slavery, taxation, education, and other issues. A crisis became imminent in 1859 when abolitionist John Brown and his followers seized the federal arsenal at Harpers Ferry. This attempt to incite a slave uprising was a prelude to the Civil War, and resulted in Brown's execution in Charleston.

Abolitionist John Brown was convinced that direct military action was the only means by which slavery could be eliminated from the United States. He led violent anti-slavery factions in Kansas during the 1850s and was captured by Robert E. Lee after his raid at Harper's Ferry. Brown was hanged for treason on December 2, 1859.

A view of Wheeling in 1854. The city was an important commercial and political center during the Civil War era and was designated the state capital in 1863.

The Civil War made West Virginia a state. After the Commonwealth of Virginia left the Union in April 1861, representatives of the western counties, which had opposed secession, held a series of meetings. In the Second Wheeling Convention, these representatives adopted a Declaration of Rights that branded the secession ordinance

illegal and reorganized state government as the Restored Government of Virginia. That August the western counties approved the formation of a new state, originally named Kanawha. The name was later changed to West Virginia, which was admitted as the 35th state in 1863, with its capital at Wheeling.

However, West Virginia was not without Confederate sympathizers, two of whom would play dramatic roles in the Civil War: General Thomas J. "Stonewall" Jackson and Belle Boyd, the renowned Confederate spy. Some 8,000 West Virginians fought for the South, while 30,000 joined Union forces. Extended conflict occurred at Philippi in April 1861, in a clash for control of the Baltimore and Ohio Railroad. Throughout the year and into 1862, federal forces under Generals George McClellan and William S. Rosecrans drove Confederate raiders back into Virginia. The town of Romney changed hands 56 times during the course of the war.

Virginia asked West Virginia to reunite with it after the war ended, but West Virginia refused. The war had left West Virginia a new state, but one in turmoil. Ruined property, heavy debt, and residual bitterness hampered recovery. Returning Confederate veterans were denied the vote until 1871.

The development of railroads allowed West Virginia to exploit valuable mineral and timber resources, and coal mining became a major industry. But working conditions in the mines were very bad: a single explosion in 1907 killed 361 miners. The first miners' strike for better wages and conditions was organized by the United Mine Workers in 1912. Twelve miners were killed in battles with mine guards, and the state militia had to intervene. In 1913 Governor Henry D. Hatfield proposed a guaranteed nine-hour work day and the right to organize unions, and peace was restored for a time.

World War I was a boom time for West Virginia. Its raw materials and manufactured products were essential to the war effort. But trouble in the coal fields flared up again after the war. In 1920 mine owners at Matewan locked union miners out of their jobs. Miners were evicted from their company-owned homes. Riots occurred, and 500 federal soldiers were sent in. The governor declared martial law, and armed conflict over the right to organize continued in 1921. The state indicted 543 miners for taking part in a four-day battle near Blair, and 22 of them were tried for treason against the state. Despite their acquittal, most miners left the union and many left the state.

Thomas J. "Stonewall" Jackson was born in Clarksburg when it was still part of Virginia. He secured an appointment to the U.S. Military Academy in 1842. When the Civil War broke out, Jackson joined the Confederate army and became one of its most honored military leaders.

During the Great Depression of the 1930s, the National Recovery Administration effected improvements by which mine owners shortened hours, raised wages, and improved working conditions, and the mining industry rallied. During World War II, mines and factories were humming with activity, as they turned out materials for the armed forces. The first synthetic rubber plant was established near Charleston in 1943.

After the war, the federal government took over many of the mines after a series of work stoppages. A decreased demand for coal, and automation in the mines during the 1950s, created widespread unemployment in West Virginia, and many miners left the state in search of other jobs. But the chemical and synthetic-textile industries, which used the state's coal, oil, salt, and water resources, were on the upswing. The glass and metal industries prospered. West Virginia is still in the process of diversifying its economy and making full use of its many resources, including natural gas, petroleum, building stone, and timber. Many visitors believe that its natural beauty is unsurpassed in the East, and tourism brings in well over $1 billion per year.

Pioneer children in western Virginia attended school in log cabins that also served as churches. West Virginia established a free school system in 1863, after it joined the Union. The first institutions of higher education in the region were Marshall University and West Liberty State College, both founded in 1837. Bethany College was established in 1840, and West Virginia University in 1867.

Charleston is the capital of West Virginia and its largest city. The state's chemical industry, an important component of its economy, is centered here.

The People

Most West Virginians live in rural areas, and some 36 percent of them live in towns and cities, including Charleston and Huntington. Almost all were born in the United States, to families who came originally from Germany, Great Britain, Hungary, Ireland, Italy, and Poland. The largest religious denominations in the state are the Methodists and Baptists. Roman Catholics, Presbyterians, Disciples of Christ, and Lutherans form other sizable communities.

Well-known West Virginians include Confederate general Thomas J. "Stonewall" Jackson, who earned his nickname for his strong stand at the first battle of Bull Run, or Manassas. Jackson was born in Clarksburg (formerly part of Virginia). The intrepid Belle Boyd, a native of Martinsburg, spied on Union forces for the Confederacy and was captured three times before she eloped to England with one of her former guards, an ensign in the U.S. Navy. Labor leader Walter Reuther, of the United Auto Workers Union, was a native of Wheeling, and Nobel Prize-winning novelist Pearl S. Buck, best known for *The Good Earth*, came from Hillsboro. Popular comedian Don Knotts was born in Morgantown.

Far left:
West Virginia's population is primarily rural, and its country music heritage depends upon such traditional instruments as the banjo and the fiddle.

Above:
West Virginia craftsmen still practice the art of woodcarving.

Harpers Ferry National
Historical Park.

IN HARPERS FERRY: *Harpers Ferry National Historical Park*
This West Virginia town has been restored to its condition in 1859, when John
  Brown seized the U.S. Armory.

IN PENDLETON COUNTY: *Seneca Rock*
This 1,000-foot-high landmark with its multicolored layers of rock towers over the
  valley below it.

IN EASTERN WEST VIRGINIA: *Monongahela National Forest*
An unspoiled wilderness of more than 1,600,000 acres.

NEAR WESTON: *Jackson's Mill*
General Thomas J. Jackson spent his boyhood on this frontier farm, which became
  the nation's first 4-H Club camp in 1921.

IN MORGAN COUNTY: *Berkeley Springs*
George Washington discovered the mineral springs here when he surveyed the land
  for Lord Fairfax, and the town has been a health resort since 1756.

For more information write:
TRAVEL DEVELOPMENT PROGRAM
OFFICE OF ECONOMIC & COMMUNITY DEVELOPMENT
STATE CAPITOL
CHARLESTON, WEST VIRGINIA 25305

FURTHER READING

Bailey, Bernadine. *Picture Book of West Virginia*, rev. ed. Whitman, 1980.
Carpenter, Allan. *West Virginia*, rev. ed. Childrens Press, 1979.
Fradin, Dennis B. *West Virginia in Words and Pictures*. Childrens Press, 1980.
Cometti, Elizabeth, and Summers, F. P., eds. *The Thirty-Fifth State: A
    Documentary History of West Virginia*. McClain, 1966.
Sutton, Felix. *West Virginia*. Coward, McCann & Geoghegan, 1968.
Williams, John A. *West Virginia: A Bicentennial History*. W.W. Norton, 1976.

INDEX

Numbers in Italics refer to illustrations

63

Photo Credits/Acknowledgments

Photos on pages 5, 6–7, 9, 11 (top), 12 (top right, bottom right), Washington Convention and Visitor's Association; pages 8, 10 (top), 11 (bottom), 12 (top left, bottom left), Bruce Glassman; pages 14, 16–17, 18, 19 (left), 28, 32 (right), 33, 36, 40 (bottom left), Library of Congress; page 20, R. Glassman; pages 21, 26, 27, 32 (top left), 34 (right), 41 (bottom left), 42, courtesy of The Virginia Division of Tourism; pages 29, 31, 34 (top left), 34 (right), 41 (bottom left), 38 (top left), 39, 40 (right), 41 (top row, bottom center, right), 53, 59, National Portrait Gallery; page 35, Stokes Collection/New York Public Library; pages 43, 49, Stephen J. Shaluta, Jr./Department of Commerce, State of West Virginia; pages 48, 50, 60, 62, Gerald S. Ratliff; page 61, Department of Commerce, State of West Virginia.

Cover photograph courtesy of Washington Convention and Visitor's Association.

The Publisher would like to thank Pamela Jewell of the Virginia Division of Tourism and David Fattaleh of The West Virginia Department of Commerce for their gracious assistance in the preparation of this book.